THE STILLNESS WITHIN

Finding Peace in a Chaotic World

Mr.Sathyamoorthy Buma Sridhar

ISBN: 9798340983046

Cover design by: Art Painter
Library of Congress Control Number: 2018675309
Printed in the United States of America

CONTENTS

INTRODUCTION

My journey to inner peace began in the depths of despair. Multiple times, I found myself grappling with mental illness, the weight of severe injuries and medications, and the agonizing pain of self-rejection. The pressures of family and work life felt insurmountable, leaving me feeling lost and broken. But in that darkness, a spark ignited. I turned to books, immersing myself in the worlds of mindfulness and emotional intelligence. These practices became my lifeline, offering a path towards healing and self-discovery. Through them, I began to see the world with fresh eyes, to cultivate self-compassion, and to navigate my emotions with greater awareness. With the support of modern psychiatry and the ancient techniques of mindfulness, I emerged from the depths of trauma, stronger and more resilient than ever before. "The Stillness Within" is a testament to the transformative power of these practices, a guide for anyone seeking to heal, grow, and find lasting peace within.

But my journey wasn't just about overcoming personal struggles; it was about discovering a deeper truth about the nature of peace and fulfillment. In a world that constantly urges us to do more, be more, and have more, it's easy to lose touch with the essence of who we are. "The Stillness Within" is a gentle reminder that true peace and fulfillment are not found in external achievements, but in the depths of our own being. Through mindfulness, we cultivate self-awareness, connect with our inner wisdom, and discover the profound beauty of the present moment. This book is your invitation to embrace the stillness within and discover the transformative power of mindfulness for yourself.

PREFACE

The statistics are alarming: millions worldwide struggle with mental health challenges, from anxiety and depression to burnout and overwhelm. The need for effective tools to navigate these complexities is urgent. "The Stillness With in." provides a compassionate and empowering guide to cultivating inner peace and emotional resilience. Whether you're seeking to manage stress, improve relationships, or simply live a more mindful life, this book offers a roadmap to greater well-being.

With gratitude and hope,
Sathyamoorthy Buma Sridhar
Mindfulness and Emotional Intelligence Coach
Mental Health Activist

AWARD WINNING BOOK

"The Stillness Within" is a Sahitya Sparsh Award Winner!

The Literature Times calls it "a refreshing guide for those seeking solace, peace, and emotional balance." This book offers practical tools and insights for cultivating mindfulness, managing stress, and finding inner peace in a chaotic world.

Grab your copy today and embark on a journey to greater well-being!

EBRACING MINDFULNESS

A JOURNEY OF SELF-PERSONAL REFLECTION

Personal Reflection: Mindfulness In My Corridor

One afternoon, as I sat in my corridor, observing the children's playful energy and the rhythm of my own breath, I found myself immersed in the simple act of being present. The touch of the chair against my body, the symphony of sounds from the park, and the gentle rise and fall of my chest became focal points of my awareness. In that moment, I realized that mindfulness wasn't about achieving a

state of thoughtlessness but rather cultivating a non-judgmental acceptance of my thoughts and sensations. As I let go of the need to control or analyze, a sense of relaxation washed over me, and the tensions in my body seemed to dissolve. It was as if I had stepped out of the drama of life and into a realm of profound peace. This experience taught me that the present moment is a precious gift, and by simply engaging my senses, I can tap into a deeper sense of joy and self-awareness.

Expert Perspectives on Mindfulness

Jon Kabat-Zinn's Definition: Mindfulness is the awareness that emerges when we pay attention, on purpose, in the present moment, without judgment. It's about acknowledging our thoughts and feelings without getting caught up in them.

Dr. Dan Siegel's COAL Acronym:

Curiosity: Approach mindfulness with a sense of wonder and openness to new experiences.

Openness: Embrace different approaches to mindfulness and find what works best for you.

Acceptance: Be kind to yourself and others, acknowledging imperfections without judgment.

Love: Cultivate a sense of compassion and kindness towards yourself and those around you.

Key Takeaways:

Mindfulness is about being present in the moment, not escaping from it.It's about accepting our thoughts and feelings without judgment.

Mindfulness can lead to greater self-awareness, relaxation, and inner peace.

It's a practice that can be cultivated through simple techniques like paying attention to your breath and senses.

Mindfulness is a journey of self-discovery, and there's no one right way to do it.

Remember: Mindfulness is a practice, not a destination. Be patient with yourself, and enjoy the journey of self-discovery.

EMBRACING SOLITUDE

A PATH TO SELF-DISCOVERY

Solitude, often perceived as a lonely state, can be a profound opportunity for self-understanding. Just as birds visit a lake, taking what they need before continuing their journey, we too navigate the world, seeking fulfillment and purpose. Our destinations may vary – some aspire to become CEOs, others seek love or material possessions – but ultimately, true understanding of ourselves remains the most enduring goal.

Life is a constant dance of changing needs and desires. Today's car might be tomorrow's forgotten luxury. Our cravings may never cease entirely, but recognizing their fleeting nature can liberate us from their relentless pursuit.

Simple moments, like sharing a morning coffee with my mother, offer profound beauty and connection. We often overlook the richness of such everyday experiences in our quest for grander adventures or relationships. While companionship is natural and fulfilling, the absence of a partner doesn't equate to loneliness. The love and bond I share with my mother provide solace and companionship.

Solitude, whether in prayer, meditation, or quiet contemplation, nurtures a connection to our deeper selves. It's a space for evolution, understanding, and tapping into our inner source. Embracing solitude allows us to navigate life's complexities with greater clarity and purpose.

True solitude is not isolation, but rather a conscious choice to cultivate inner peace and self-awareness. It's a journey of self-discovery, and its rewards are immeasurable. As we learn to embrace solitude, we unlock a profound sense of contentment and connection to the world around us.

A TRANQUIL EVENING STROLL

THE HEALING POWER OF NATURE

It was nearing 5 PM, the sun beginning its gentle descent, casting a warm glow over the serene lake. A refreshing breeze whispered through the air as I embarked on a leisurely walk along the water's edge. The symphony of nature surrounded me – birds chirped their melodious tunes, while trees swayed gracefully in the wind, their leaves shimmering like emeralds in the fading light.

The water, kissed by the golden hues of the setting sun, sparkled and danced, sending gentle waves to caress the shore. A few fellow strollers sat contemplatively, their gazes fixed on the rhythmic dance of fish and fishermen. Water birds darted across the surface, adding to the vibrant tapestry of life unfolding before me.

As I continued my journey, covering several kilometers along the lakeside path, a profound sense of well-being washed over me. My body felt invigorated, my once-agitated mind now calm and serene. Witnessing the harmonious interplay of nature's elements filled me with an inexplicable joy.

Inspired by this experience, I later delved into the research on the benefits of walking in nature. I discovered a wealth of evidence supporting the positive impact on both physical and mental health. From reduced stress and anxiety to improved cardiovascular health and cognitive function, the advantages were undeniable. It became clear that my tranquil lakeside stroll was not just a pleasant experience, but a powerful act of self-care.

SHIFTING FROM NEGATIVE TO POSITIVE

Reframing Your Mindset

Our minds can often become trapped in a cycle of negativity, replaying past hurts, worries, and anxieties. Thoughts like "He hurt me deeply," "That argument was terrible," or "I can't forget that conversation" can consume us, leading to negative decisions, feelings, and emotions. The more we unconsciously dwell on these thoughts, the more they shape our conscious reality.

So how do we break free from this negative frame of mind? The key lies in consciously shifting our focus towards positive memories and experiences.

Acknowledge and Accept: The first step is to acknowledge the negative thoughts without judgment. Recognize that they are present, but don't let them control you.

Consciously Redirect: When negative thoughts arise, consciously redirect your attention to positive memories. Recall joyful moments, achievements, and experiences that bring you happiness.

Cultivate Gratitude: Practice gratitude by focusing on the good things in your life. This helps to shift your perspective and create a more positive outlook.

Mindfulness and Meditation: Engage in mindfulness practices and meditation to cultivate present-moment awareness and reduce the power of negative thoughts.

Examples of Positive Reframing:

Instead of dwelling on a past hurt, remember a time when you felt loved and supported.

Instead of focusing on a recent argument, recall a happy memory with your partner.

Instead of replaying a negative conversation, remember a beautiful moment in nature or a personal accomplishment.

Remember, happiness is a choice. By consciously cultivating positive thoughts and memories, we can rewire our minds and create a more fulfilling and joyful life.

I was spending time with special children last month they were so kind to me!

You can frame your sentence, probably you can journal your good memories!

THE POWER OF PERCEPTION

AND LIFELONG LEARNING

Pavlov's famous experiment with dogs demonstrated the concept of "conditioned response." By associating a bell with food, he conditioned the dogs to salivate at the sound of the bell alone, even without the presence of food. This

highlights the profound influence of associations and memories on our behavior and perceptions.

The Illusion of Perception: Good and Bad

Similarly, our minds can be conditioned to perceive people, products, or situations based on past experiences or external influences. A kind person might be misjudged as cruel due to a single negative encounter, or a harmful product might be perceived as beneficial due to clever marketing.

Mindful Non-Judgmental Witnessing

To overcome these conditioned responses and see reality clearly, we need to cultivate mindful non-judgmental witnessing. This involves observing without preconceived notions or biases, allowing us to understand the true nature of things.

The Importance of Lifelong Learning

Learning should be a continuous process throughout our lives. The willingness to learn from every experience, even mistakes, allows us to adapt, grow, and make informed decisions.

Mindful Learning and New Perspectives

Mindful learning opens doors to new dimensions and perspectives. It challenges our assumptions and helps us see the world with fresh eyes, leading to better decision-making and a more fulfilling life.

Avoiding Stagnation

The belief that we have learned everything can lead to stagnation and missed opportunities. Embracing a mindset of continuous learning keeps us open to new possibilities and ensures we never stop growing.

Conclusion

By understanding the power of conditioning and cultivating mindful non-judgmental witnessing, we can break free from limiting beliefs and see the world as it truly is. Embracing lifelong learning allows us to adapt, evolve, and make informed decisions, leading to a more fulfilling and meaningful life.

THE PERILS OF AUTOPILOT

AND THE POWER OF MINDFUL AWARENESS

Living on autopilot, we miss the richness of life, physically present yet mentally absent. Without awareness, we fail to truly see and experience the events unfolding around us. We miss opportunities for connection, understanding, and growth.

True listening requires attention and awareness. Only then can we grasp the nuances of communication, recognize our own biases, and understand the perspectives of others.

Prejudice flourishes in the absence of mindfulness. Assuming we know everything without validating our beliefs against reality creates a distorted lens that colors our perceptions and decisions. This can have devastating consequences, leading to misjudgments, missed opportunities, and unnecessary suffering.

Mindful awareness allows us to step back from our preconceived notions and observe the present moment with clarity and openness. It helps us recognize the intricacies of life, challenge our assumptions, and avoid the pitfalls of prejudice. By being fully present, we can navigate life's complexities with greater wisdom and compassion.

Without mindful awareness, we risk living in a state of delusion, reacting to life based on outdated beliefs and assumptions. We miss the opportunity to learn, grow, and evolve.

Cultivating mindful present-moment awareness is essential for addressing prejudices and living a more authentic and fulfilling life. It allows us to see the world as it truly is, free from the distortions of our own minds. Embrace the power of mindfulness and unlock the potential for a richer, more meaningful existence.

NAVIGATING LIFE'S COMPLEXITIES

*UNDERSTANDING OUR
DECISIONS AND BEHAVIORS*

Why he behaves with me like that? Sometimes we use to think like that, have you noticed in yourself? If we watch us closely every time we take some decision, we think at the surface level or deeper aspect also. Based on our decision our behavior varies, some timing impact of the situation is serious or vary lighter, on the whole, we make a decision in some form.

Life is a combination of Acts we do; we have to be very careful about every act we do. When we behave normally or sometimes, we behave sarcastically we never worry about the act or behavior.

When we start analyzing how we take the decision and act we will come to know our character.

In normal life in the ordinary situation, we behave casually, and we take more decisions, our mother asks you what to cook tomorrow for office you think and tell some interesting dish. Likewise, mind take the decision normally indifferent situations. When we confused our decision will impact our behavior and character. Based on the confusing situation how we take the decision determines our success. We doubt our behavior when we are confused. we tell crisis, situation, and time for the decision you make. We need to understand our process according to the situation, "I have more tension... I am having a sleeping tablet" If someone tells you what you think? On the surface he doesn't have sleep so he has tablets if we think deeply having a tablet is a temporary measure for confusion or imbalance in the mind. Understanding the problem and addressing could be a better solution. When you had an accident in your leg, you might bleed with blood, instead of going through the pain and worrying for that pain, you should have the right process to deal with the pain. you go to the better doctor to clean the blood, protect the wound with medicine will be right process to handle the situation.

Have you ever found yourself questioning someone else's actions, wondering, "Why do they behave that way towards me?" It's a common experience, but have you ever turned that question inward? Our own decisions and behaviors are often driven by complex factors, both conscious and unconscious.

The Anatomy of Decision-Making

Every action we take stems from a decision, whether made thoughtfully or impulsively. The impact of our choices can range from trivial to life-altering. In ordinary situations, our minds make decisions effortlessly, like choosing a meal for tomorrow's lunch. However, in moments of confusion, our decision-making process becomes more intricate, influencing our behavior and shaping our character.

Confusion and its Consequences

Confusion can cloud our judgment and lead to impulsive actions. We may resort to quick fixes, like taking a sleeping pill to escape insomnia, instead of addressing the root cause of our sleeplessness. Just as treating a bleeding wound requires proper medical attention, addressing the underlying cause of our confusion is crucial for long-term well-being.

The Path to Clarity

Navigating confusion requires a thoughtful approach. Consider the example of loving your partner while facing a job crisis. Relocating for a new job may satisfy your financial needs, but it could strain your relationship. The key is to assess your priorities and make decisions that align with your long-term goals.

Understanding Our Evolving Needs

Our needs change throughout life, influenced by age, circumstances, and personal growth. The carefree desires of youth may give way to the responsibilities of adulthood, parenthood, and career aspirations. Recognizing these shifts allows us to adapt our decision-making processes accordingly.

Taking Ownership and Making Informed Choices

Taking ownership of our lives requires aligning our thoughts and actions. It's crucial to ensure our needs are reasonable and our decisions are based on careful consideration, not impulsive desires. We must weigh the present against the future, avoiding short-term solutions that create long-term problems.

A Framework for Navigating Confusion:

Thorough Understanding: Gain a deep understanding of the situation at hand.

Identify Wants and Needs: Clearly define what you truly want and need.

Consider Future Growth: Make decisions that support your long-term goals.

Address Root Causes: Seek permanent solutions, not just temporary fixes.

Avoid Impulsive Decisions: Don't make decisions in moments of anger, stress, or compulsion.

Assess Your Capacity: Ensure you can handle the potential outcomes of your decision.

Stay Grounded: Avoid being swayed by unrealistic dreams or expectations.

Prioritize Inner Peace: Choose actions that promote calmness and well-being.

Learn from the Past: Use past experiences and mistakes to guide your choices.

Seek Feedback: Be open to receiving and considering feedback from trusted individuals.

By following these guidelines and cultivating mindful awareness, we can navigate life's complexities with greater clarity, wisdom, and inner peace. Remember, every decision is an opportunity for growth and self-discovery.

NAVIGATING

*THE COMPLEXITIES OF
LOVE AND LOSS*

The echoes of past love can linger, shaping our present relationships and influencing our emotional well-being. Memories of deep connections and tender moments can be both cherished and painful, making it challenging to move forward.

In the tapestry of human relationships, we encounter diverse characters and dynamics. Some approach love with an immature exuberance, unaware of its potential complexities. Others, burdened by past heartbreaks, struggle to open themselves to new possibilities, trapped in a cycle of grief and longing.

Then there are those who embody maturity and understanding. They recognize the power of acceptance and patience, offering a safe space for healing and growth. They understand that love requires more than just passion; it demands compassion, empathy, and the willingness to let go of the past.

Our roles in life's intricate dance are not fixed. We can choose to embody the qualities we admire, to embrace love with tenderness and understanding, and to navigate the complexities of relationships with grace and compassion. By acknowledging the past without clinging to it, we create space for new connections and experiences.

Dwelling on past hurts or anxieties about the future can lead to psychological distress. It's essential to cultivate present-moment awareness and acceptance, allowing ourselves to fully experience the joys and challenges of the present.

When we communicate our pain and boundaries with compassion, we offer others a chance to understand and grow. By choosing empathy over resentment, we foster healing and create opportunities for stronger connections.

Conversely, clinging to past wounds and harboring resentment can breed conflict and erode our mental well-being. Unresolved emotions can manifest as anxiety, depression, and strained relationships. It's crucial to recognize the impact of our choices on ourselves and those around us.

Ultimately, embracing acceptance, letting go of the past, cultivating compassion, and developing present-moment awareness are key to fostering healthy relationships and inner peace. By embodying these qualities, we create a foundation for a fulfilling and meaningful life, both within ourselves and in connection with others.

THE BATTLE WITHIN

*ANXIETY AND THE QUEST FOR
PRESENT- MOMENT AWARENESS*

Life can often feel like a battle, especially when we become consumed by worries about future events. The anticipation of an upcoming presentation, a crucial job interview, or even a joyous occasion like the arrival of a new car can trigger a cascade of stress hormones in our bodies. These physiological responses can disrupt our sleep, leaving us feeling agitated and restless.

Imagine a child eagerly awaiting the delivery of a new car. The excitement builds, consuming their thoughts and making sleep elusive. They envision the car arriving, plan their grand welcome, and perhaps even dream of future adventures behind the wheel. This anticipation, while joyful, can also create a sense of anxiety and restlessness.

Similarly, adults experience varying degrees of anxiety in response to future events. The intensity of this anxiety can range from mild excitement to debilitating panic. When these feelings persist and interfere with our daily lives, they may signal a deeper issue.

Mindfulness emerges as a powerful tool in managing anxiety. By cultivating present-moment awareness, we can anchor ourselves in the here and now, reducing the grip of worries about the future. Through practices like meditation, deep breathing, and mindful observation, we can learn to acknowledge our anxieties without becoming overwhelmed by them.

It's important to distinguish between normal anxiety and anxiety disorders. While occasional anxiety is a natural human experience, anxiety disorders involve persistent and excessive worry that significantly impairs daily functioning. If you suspect you may be struggling with an anxiety disorder, seeking professional help from a psychiatrist is crucial.

Remember, mindfulness can be a valuable ally in managing everyday anxieties. By cultivating present-moment awareness, you can regain control of your thoughts and emotions, promoting a greater sense of calm and well-being. However, if anxiety becomes overwhelming or interferes with your life, don't hesitate to reach out to a mental health professional for support and guidance.

EMBRACING SOLITUDE

*FINDING CONTENTMENT IN
THE ART OF BEING ALONE*

In the hustle and bustle of our daily lives, we often find ourselves surrounded by people, responsibilities, and distractions. But what happens when the noise fades, and we are left with only ourselves? This is the story of a man who faced the unexpected challenge of unemployment and the accompanying loneliness.

At first, the newfound freedom felt liberating. He enjoyed the absence of deadlines and pressures. Yet, as days turned into weeks, the initial euphoria gave way to boredom and frustration. Despite having his basic needs met, he felt a profound sense of emptiness. He was lonely and unsure of how to spend his time in a meaningful way.

One day, amidst his growing discontent, he paused and asked himself a simple yet powerful question: "Why am I sad?" The answer came to him with surprising clarity: he was idle, without work or companionship. This realization marked a turning point. He began to explore his hobbies and interests, seeking ways to fill his days with purpose and joy, even in solitude.

As he delved deeper into his passions, he rediscovered a sense of fulfillment. He learned to appreciate the quiet moments, to embrace the beauty of his own company. The loneliness that once haunted him gradually transformed into a sense of contentment and self-reliance.

This story teaches us a valuable lesson: the importance of understanding ourselves and learning to manage loneliness. While we may thrive in the company of others, there will inevitably be times in our lives when we find ourselves alone. Whether it's due to retirement, a change in circumstances, or simply the natural ebb and flow of life, solitude is an unavoidable reality.

By cultivating the art of being alone, we equip ourselves to navigate these inevitable periods with grace and resilience. We learn to find joy in our own company, to pursue our passions, and to appreciate the simple pleasures of life.

Remember, even in the midst of a bustling career or a fulfilling social life, the ability to be alone is a valuable asset. It allows us to recharge, reflect, and connect with our deepest selves. So, embrace solitude, not as a burden, but as an opportunity for growth and self-discovery.

THE RHYTHM
OF HEALING

FINDING JOY IN THE DJEMBE DRUM

A veil of sadness had settled over me, its weight pulling me down into a state of worry and despair. The reasons for my melancholy were numerous, a tangled web of thoughts and emotions that clouded my mind. But amidst the darkness, a flicker of hope remained. I yearned for happiness and joy, determined to make choices that would lead me towards a brighter path.

When our emotions threaten to drown us in sorrow, we must find ways to lift ourselves back into the light. Music, with its ability to evoke powerful feelings and shift our perspectives, can be a potent source of solace and healing. And so, I turned to the rhythmic pulse of the djembe drum, seeking refuge in its vibrant beats.

As my hands struck the drumhead, a transformation began. The sadness that once consumed me started to dissipate, replaced by a sense of focus and connection. The vibrations resonated through my body, stirring a dormant energy within. With each beat, I felt a release, a shedding of the burdens that had weighed me down.

Research supports the therapeutic benefits of drumming. Studies have shown that playing the djembe drum can decrease levels of cortisol, the stress hormone, promoting a sense of calm and well-being. It's a powerful tool for fostering emotional release and facilitating a shift towards a more positive frame of mind.

The communal nature of drumming adds another layer of healing. As Robert Lawrence Friedman, a psychotherapist and drumming advocate, points out, "It's the only instrument that allows a lot of people to speak at once." In a world dominated by technology and isolation, drumming offers a way to connect with others on a primal level, fostering a sense of belonging and shared experience.

Friedman and others believe that group drumming serves as a form of nonverbal communication, transcending words and tapping into deeper emotional states. This unique form of expression has proven effective in therapeutic settings, helping individuals of all ages, from troubled teens to elderly patients with Alzheimer's, to connect with their emotions and improve their well-being.

My experience with the djembe drum taught me the profound power of music to heal and uplift. It reminded me that even in the darkest moments, we have the ability to choose joy. By embracing creative outlets like drumming, we can shift our emotional states, cultivate positivity, and rediscover the vibrant rhythm of life.

FROM MINDFULNESS
TO TRANSCENDENCE

A JOURNEY OF LOVE
AND GRATITUDE

Sitting in the corridor, I embarked on a journey of heightened awareness. With each breath, I observed the subtle movements of my senses, naming and acknowledging the sensations that arose. Gradually, my focus deepened, and I delved into a space where only the rhythm of my breath remained.

In this state of profound stillness, I became aware of my root chakra, a wellspring of energy and vitality. From this center, I expressed love and gratitude, allowing these emotions to flow through me and permeate every aspect of my being.

With each chakra receiving this infusion of love, my awareness expanded, seeking to encompass every cell in my body. I showered my cells with love, recognizing their intricate role in sustaining my life and well-being.

Beyond the physical realm, my awareness extended further, seeking to connect with the five elements that form the foundation of existence. Earth, water, fire, air, and space – I expressed my love and gratitude for their presence and their contribution to the symphony of life.

In this state of profound connection, I transcended the

boundaries of my individual self. My awareness merged with the boundless expanse of creation, and I experienced a sense of oneness with the universe. I expressed my love to myself, to the divine source of all creation, and to the interconnectedness of all things.

Gradually, I returned to my ordinary state of awareness, carrying with me the echoes of this transcendent experience.

Observations:

I journeyed from a state of mindfulness to a state of deep meditation.

I expressed love and gratitude to my body, mind, soul, the five elements, and the divine source of all creation.

I experienced a profound sense of oneness and interconnectedness.

This experience left me filled with a deep sense of peace and gratitude. It reminded me of the boundless potential for love and connection that exists within us and all around us.

Key takeaways:

Through mindfulness and meditation, we can access deeper states of awareness and connection.

Expressing love and gratitude can foster a sense of well-being and oneness with the universe.

Transcendent experiences can offer profound insights and a deeper understanding of ourselves and our place in the world.

THE INNER BATTLE

CULTIVATING PRESENT- MOMENT AWARENESS AND HEALING TRAUMA

For many, the journey toward inner awareness feels like an uphill battle. The constant chatter of the mind, filled with worries about the past, present, and future, can make it challenging to truly connect with our inner selves and experience the richness of the present moment.

We long to feel our senses deeply, to cultivate a profound connection with our bodies and emotions. Yet, the incessant stream of thoughts acts as a barrier, pulling us away from the core of our being. It's a struggle to silence the noise and simply be present.

Past traumas, whether recent or long-buried, can further complicate this journey. The pain and fear associated with these experiences can create a sense of disconnection, making it difficult to access our inner strength and wisdom. We may find ourselves trapped in cycles of avoidance and distraction, seeking to numb the pain rather than face it.

But amidst the chaos, there is hope. By embracing practices that foster mindfulness and self-compassion, we can gradually heal our wounds and reconnect with our true essence. Mindful breathing, for example, anchors us in the present moment, allowing us to observe our thoughts and emotions without judgment. Practicing gratitude shifts our focus towards the positive aspects of our lives, cultivating a sense of appreciation and abundance.

Prayer and meditation offer pathways to deeper connection with our inner selves and the divine. These practices can help us transcend the limitations of the mind and tap into a wellspring of peace and wisdom.

The journey towards inner awareness is not always easy, but it is a worthwhile pursuit. By cultivating present-moment awareness and embracing practices that promote healing and self-compassion, we can overcome the challenges of trauma, quiet the noise of the mind, and experience the profound joy of connecting with our true selves.

UNRAVELING THE FURY

Anger Defined:
Anger is that potent emotion that surges within us when we perceive someone's actions as unjust, cruel, or simply unacceptable. It's a visceral reaction, a fiery storm that can consume us entirely.

The True Cost of Anger:

While anger may seem like a justified response to mistreatment, it's crucial to recognize the hidden toll it takes on us. When we succumb to anger, we become the primary victims. Our emotional well-being suffers, our minds and bodies are flooded with stress hormones, and we perpetuate a cycle of pain and frustration.

The Lingering Impact:

The person who wronged us may move on, oblivious to the turmoil they've caused. But for us, the anger festers, clouding our thoughts and hindering our ability to find peace. We become trapped in a self-inflicted prison of resentment and bitterness.

The Path to Liberation:

True liberation from anger comes when we realize that it no longer serves us. It's a moment of clarity, an understanding that holding onto anger only perpetuates our own suffering. As we begin to accept the reality of the situation, the grip of anger loosens, and we can finally begin to heal.

The Roots of Anger:

To understand anger is to embark on a journey of self-discovery. Anger often arises when our expectations clash with reality. We create an idealized image of how things should be, and when events or people deviate from this script, we react with anger.

Acceptance and Letting Go:

The antidote to anger lies in acceptance. When we learn to accept situations as they are, without judgment or resistance, we create space for peace and understanding. By releasing our expectations and embracing the present moment, we can navigate life's challenges with greater equanimity.

Conclusion:

Anger is a powerful emotion that can cause significant harm to ourselves and our relationships. By understanding its origins and cultivating acceptance, we can break free from its grasp and create a more peaceful and fulfilling life. Remember, true strength lies not in reacting with anger, but in responding with wisdom and compassion.

EMBRACING FEAR

Childhood, a time of boundless energy and playful exploration, can also be a breeding ground for fears and anxieties. The young boy cycling home from tuition in the darkness, his heart pounding with the fear of snakes and imagined ghosts, embodies this universal experience. Though the threats may not have been real, the fear was palpable, impacting his well-being and sense of security.

But within this fear lay the seeds of transformation. As the boy realized the futility of his anxieties and focused on his aspirations for a successful future, he gradually faced his fears head-on. By accepting the reality of his situation and embracing a sense of purpose, he transcended his fear, his heartbeat returning to its normal rhythm.

Fear, in its various forms, touches us all. We fear rejection, failure, the unknown, and countless other perceived threats. These fears often stem from a lack of understanding and an inability to face the potential consequences of unfamiliar situations.

But can we learn to accept fear rather than succumb to it? Can we confront the unknown with courage and clarity? The answer lies in cultivating mindfulness and a willingness to observe our fears without judgment.

When we acknowledge our fear and remain watchful, a profound shift occurs. Fear gives way to alertness, and our heightened awareness empowers us to navigate challenging situations with newfound courage. Our heartbeat may still quicken, but it is no longer driven by panic; it is a sign of our readiness to face whatever lies ahead.

By embracing fear and understanding its nature, we tap into a wellspring of inner strength. We become fearless, not because we are immune to fear, but because we have learned to harness its energy and transform it into courage.

The journey from childhood anxieties to fearless living is a testament to the transformative power of self-awareness and acceptance. By confronting our fears and embracing the unknown, we can unlock our true potential and live life to the fullest.

CULTIVATING CALMNESS AND JOY

In the quest for inner peace and well-being, we often seek external solutions, overlooking the profound power that lies within our own minds. One simple yet effective way to cultivate calmness and joy is to tap into the reservoir of happy memories and past achievements stored within our brains.

The Alpha Wave Connection:

Research suggests that recalling positive experiences can trigger the generation of alpha waves in the brain. These brainwaves are associated with a relaxed and meditative state, promoting feelings of calmness and contentment. By consciously revisiting happy memories, we can actively induce this state of tranquility.

A Bedtime Ritual for Inner Peace:

Before drifting off to sleep, take a few moments to reflect on the highlights of your day or week. Recall moments of joy, laughter, and connection. Relive past accomplishments and savor the sense of pride and satisfaction they evoked. As you immerse yourself in these positive memories, your brain will naturally shift into a more relaxed and peaceful state, preparing you for a restful night's sleep.

Prayer and Meditation:

Incorporating prayer or meditation into your bedtime routine can further enhance your sense of inner peace. These practices provide an opportunity to connect with your spiritual beliefs, express gratitude, and let go of any lingering worries or anxieties.

A Word of Caution:

While reflecting on past achievements can be empowering, it's important to maintain a balanced perspective. Avoid dwelling on past successes to the point of arrogance or complacency. Remember that the present moment holds new opportunities for growth and learning.

Conclusion:

Cultivating calmness and joy is an ongoing practice. By harnessing the power of positive memories, prayer, and meditation, we can create a bedtime ritual that promotes relaxation, reduces anxiety, and sets the stage for a more peaceful and fulfilling life.

THE POWER OF
THE PEN

*JOURNALING FOR MENTAL
WELL-BEING*

Remember those teenage years, when a hidden diary served as a confidante, a safe space to pour out your deepest fears and anxieties? The simple act of transferring those swirling thoughts and emotions onto paper brought clarity and relief. While the diary may have been tucked away with adulthood, the concept and its benefits remain as relevant as ever. Today, we call it journaling, but the essence is the same: putting pen to paper to explore the landscape of our inner world. For those grappling with stress, depression, or anxiety, journaling can be a lifeline. It's a tool for gaining control over emotions and nurturing mental health.

When life throws curveballs, journaling helps you identify the root causes of your stress and anxiety. By pinpointing these triggers, you can develop strategies to tackle them head-on, paving the way for a less stressful existence. Remember, journaling is just one piece of the puzzle. A healthy lifestyle, encompassing exercise, balanced nutrition, and adequate sleep, is also crucial for managing stress, anxiety, and mental health challenges.

Personally, I find solace in my nightly writing ritual. I prefer the term "expressing" to "journaling" because it captures the raw honesty of the process. Whether it's happiness, sadness, intellectual musings, or deep-seated worries, I pour it all onto the page. It's a private conversation with myself, a safe haven for emotions that might be difficult to share with others.

The act of expressing myself brings a sense of release and clarity. Tensions dissipate, worries lose their grip, and a meditative calm descends. It's as if the weight of the world lifts, leaving me feeling lighter and more at peace.

Key Takeaways:

Journaling offers a safe and private space for emotional expression.It helps identify stressors and develop coping strategies.The act of writing can promote clarity, reduce anxiety, and foster a sense of calm.

Journaling complements a healthy lifestyle for improved mental well-being.It's a personal journey of self-discovery and emotional release.

Embrace the power of the pen. Let your thoughts and feelings flow freely onto the page, and discover the transformative potential of journaling for your mental health.

THE HEALING

My Neighbor, My Mother, And The Unforeseen Argument

One evening, a seemingly trivial incident escalated into a heated confrontation between my neighbor and my

mother. His disrespectful tone and disregard for her age triggered a wave of anger within me. I intervened, but the damage was done. My mother felt deeply hurt, and I, too, couldn't shake off the lingering resentment.

The neighbor's words echoed in my mind, robbing me of sleep and inner peace. I realized that holding onto this anger was only causing me further pain. It was time to seek a resolution, not through retaliation, but through the transformative power of forgiveness.

Understanding Forgiveness

Forgiveness is not about condoning hurtful actions or forgetting the past. It's about consciously choosing to release the burden of resentment and reclaim your inner peace. It's a journey of healing and self-liberation.

Feeling Your Pain

Acknowledging and honoring your pain is crucial. Notice where you feel it in your body and ask yourself what you need in that moment. Perhaps it's support, time, or self-care. Allowing space for the pain helps you gauge your readiness to let go.

Identify the emotions that surface as you consider forgiveness. It might be guilt, grief, shame, sorrow, confusion, or anger. Recognizing these feelings is the first step towards healing.

Expressing Your Hurt

Bottling up hurt feelings only intensifies their impact. Find healthy outlets for expression, whether it's journaling, talking to a trusted friend, or seeking professional guidance. Sharing your experience can offer new perspectives and facilitate healing.

Shifting Perspectives

Try to see the situation from the other person's point of view. Consider their life experiences and the factors that may have contributed to their hurtful actions. This doesn't excuse their behavior, but it can foster compassion and understanding.

Taking Action

Taking small steps towards forgiveness can empower you. Write a letter, have a difficult conversation, or engage in a gesture of kindness. These actions, though challenging, can lead to a sense of closure and healing.

Remembering You're Not Alone

Recognize that you're not the first or last person to experience hurt and betrayal. Making mistakes is part of the human condition. Remembering this can help lessen the grip of resentment.

Taking small steps towards forgiveness can empower you. Write a letter, have a difficult conversation, or engage in a gesture of kindness. These actions, though challenging, can lead to a sense of closure and healing.

Patience and Practice

Forgiveness is a process that unfolds over time. Be patient with yourself, especially when dealing with deep wounds. Start with smaller transgressions and gradually work your way towards forgiving more significant hurts.

Letting Go of Blame

While venting can offer temporary relief, blaming others keeps us trapped in negativity. Focus on taking responsibility for your own healing and well-being.

Cultivating Mindfulness

Mindfulness strengthens our capacity for forgiveness. By observing our thoughts and emotions without judgment, we create space for compassion and understanding.

Finding Meaning and Strength

Even in the face of pain, we can find meaning and cultivate resilience. Embrace the opportunity to grow stronger through self-compassion, courage, and empathy.

A Mini Forgiveness Practice

Try this simple exercise to strengthen your forgiveness muscles. Visualize a past hurt, acknowledge the pain it caused, and observe the emotions and thoughts that arise. If you're ready, silently repeat: "Breathing in, I acknowledge the pain. Breathing out, I am forgiving and releasing this burden from my heart and mind."

By embracing forgiveness, we free ourselves from the chains of resentment and create space for healing, growth, and inner peace. Redit to Source for practicing Mindful Forgiveness:

THE ART OF MINDFUL SURRENDER

FINDING BALANCE BETWEEN EFFORT AND ACCEPTANCE

In a world that glorifies relentless pursuit and tireless striving, the notion of surrender can seem counterintuitive. We're taught to "reach for the moon" and "never give up," associating surrender with weakness and defeat. However, true surrender, when practiced mindfully, can be an empowering act of acceptance and self-trust.

The Illusion of Control

We often cling to the belief that we can control every aspect of our lives. But the truth is, much of what unfolds is beyond our grasp. Desperate attempts to force outcomes can lead to anxiety, burnout, and disappointment. It's like trying to hold sand tightly in your fist - the harder you squeeze, the more it slips away.

The Paradox of Effort and Surrender

Mindful surrender is not about giving up on your dreams or abandoning your efforts. It's about recognizing the limitations of control and embracing the uncertainty of life. It's about trusting the journey, even when the destination is unclear.Like a bird soaring through the sky, we need both the power of our wings and the wisdom to glide on the currents of life. We must learn to balance intentional effort with mindful surrender, recognizing when to push forward and when to let go.

The Serenity Prayer

The Serenity Prayer offers a timeless reminder of this delicate balance: "Grant me the serenity to accept the things I cannot change, courage to change the things I can, and wisdom to know the difference."

Serenity: The ability to remain calm and centered amidst change and uncertainty.

Courage: The strength to face challenges and make difficult choices.

Wisdom: The discernment to recognize what is within our control and what is not.

Embracing the Present Moment

Worrying about the future or dwelling on the past robs us of the present moment. Mindful surrender allows us to fully experience the here and now, appreciating the beauty and opportunities that surround us.

From Limitation to Liberation

Surrender is not a sign of weakness, but a gateway to liberation. By releasing our attachment to specific outcomes, we open ourselves to new possibilities and experiences. We move from a place of limitation to a space of unlimited potential.

The Dance of Effort and Surrender

Striving for our goals and surrendering to the flow of life are not mutually exclusive. They are two sides of the same coin, both essential for a fulfilling and successful journey.

The Rewards of Mindful Surrender

When we find the balance between effort and surrender, we tap into a deeper sense of self-awareness and fulfillment. We learn to enjoy the journey, embrace the unknown, and trust that the best is yet to come.

Conclusion

Mindful surrender is not about giving up; it's about letting go of the illusion of control and embracing the wisdom of acceptance. By finding the delicate balance between effort and surrender, we can navigate life's complexities with grace, resilience, and a profound sense of inner peace.

MINDFUL MOMENTS

*WEAVING AWARENESS
INTO EVERYDAY LIFE*

In our fast-paced world, mindfulness can easily become another task on our to-do list, something we squeeze in between meetings or chores. But the true essence of mindfulness lies in its integration into our daily routines. By infusing everyday activities with awareness, we can transform mundane moments into opportunities for presence and connection.

Mindful Eating:

Slow Down and Savor: Instead of rushing through meals, take the time to truly savor each bite. Notice the flavors, textures, and aromas of your food. Chew slowly and deliberately, paying attention to the sensations in your mouth and body.

Engage Your Senses: Put away distractions and focus on the present experience of eating. Notice the colors, shapes, and presentation of your food. Listen to the sounds of chewing and swallowing.

Gratitude and Appreciation: Cultivate a sense of gratitude for the nourishment your food provides. Appreciate the effort that went into growing, preparing, and serving your meal.

Mindful Walking:

Feel Your Feet: Pay attention to the sensations of your feet making contact with the ground. Notice the shifting of your weight, the muscles engaging, and the rhythm of your steps.

Observe Your Surroundings: Take in the sights, sounds, and smells of your environment. Notice the trees, the sky, the people passing by. Be curious and open to the world around you.

Let Go of Thoughts: If your mind wanders, gently bring your attention back to the present moment. Don't judge yourself for getting distracted; simply acknowledge the thoughts and return to your walking meditation.

Mindful Working:

Pause and Breathe: Take short breaks throughout your workday to pause and breathe deeply. Notice the rise and fall of your chest, the sensation of air entering and leaving your nostrils.

Focus on One Task at a Time: Resist the urge to multitask. Instead, focus your full attention on one task at a time. This will improve your concentration and reduce stress.

Set Intentions: Before starting a task, set a clear intention for what you want to accomplish. This will help you stay focused and motivated.

Mindful Communication: Listen actively and speak with intention. Pay attention to your words and body language, and be present in your interactions with colleagues.

Remember:

Start Small: Begin by incorporating mindfulness into one or two activities each day. Gradually expand your practice as it becomes more natural.

Be Patient and Kind: Don't judge yourself if your mind wanders.

Simply notice the thoughts and gently bring your attention back to the present moment.

Embrace the Journey: Mindfulness is a lifelong practice. Enjoy the process of cultivating greater awareness and presence in your daily life. By weaving mindfulness into everyday activities, we can create a more peaceful, joyful, and fulfilling life.

EXPLORING

*How Mindfulness can enhance
Creativity and Problem-Solving Skill*

In a world that demands constant adaptation and innovation, the ability to think creatively and solve problems effectively has become more valuable than ever. While we often associate creativity with spontaneous bursts of inspiration, it is, in fact,

a skill that can be cultivated and enhanced through mindful practices.

The Mindful Advantage:

Mindfulness, by its very nature, encourages us to approach life with openness, curiosity, and non-judgmental awareness.

These qualities create fertile ground for creative thinking and problem-solving. When we are fully present in the moment, we can tap into our intuition and access a deeper well of ideas and solutions.

Enhanced Focus And Concentration:

Mindfulness meditation has been shown to improve focus and concentration, essential skills for tackling complex problems and generating creative solutions. By training our minds to stay anchored in the present moment, we can filter out distractions and direct our attention towards the task at hand.

Openness To New Perspectives:

Mindfulness fosters a non-judgmental attitude towards our thoughts and experiences. This openness allows us to explore unconventional ideas and perspectives, leading to innovative solutions and breakthroughs.

Reduced Stress And Anxiety:

Stress and anxiety can stifle creativity and cloud our judgment. Mindfulness helps us manage these emotions, creating a more relaxed and receptive mental state conducive to creative exploration.

Increased Self-Awareness:

Through mindful self-observation, we gain insights into our thought patterns, habits, and emotional triggers. This self-awareness empowers us to identify and overcome mental blocks that may hinder our creativity.

Embracing The "Beginner's Mind"

Mindfulness encourages us to approach each experience with fresh eyes, like a beginner encountering something for the first time. This "beginner's mind" cultivates curiosity and openness, essential ingredients for creative problem-solving.

The Creative Process And Mindfulness:

Preparation: Mindfulness meditation can enhance divergent thinking, a key component of brainstorming and idea generation.

Incubation: Mindfulness can help us step back and allow ideas to simmer in our subconscious, leading to unexpected insights and breakthroughs.

Illumination: When the "aha!" moment arrives, mindfulness ensures we are present and receptive to receive it.

Verification: Mindfulness helps us evaluate ideas objectively and make informed decisions.

Practical Tips for Integrating Mindfulness into Creative Work: Mindful Breaks: Take short mindfulness breaks throughout your workday to clear your mind and recharge your creative energy.

Mindful Observation: Pay close attention to your surroundings and experiences, noticing details that might spark new ideas.

Mindful Journaling: Use journaling to capture fleeting thoughts and insights, fostering a deeper connection with your creative self.

Mindful Collaboration: Practice active listening and open communication when working with others, fostering a collaborative and creative environment.

By embracing mindfulness, we can tap into our innate creativity and problem-solving abilities. Whether you're an artist, a writer, an entrepreneur, or simply seeking to navigate life's challenges with greater ease and ingenuity, mindfulness offers a powerful pathway to unlocking your creative potential.

THE SCIENCE OF STILLNESS

*HOW MINDFULNESS REWIRES
YOUR BRAIN AND BODY*

While mindfulness has ancient roots in contemplative traditions, modern science has increasingly validated its profound impact on our physical and mental well-being. Numerous studies have illuminated the remarkable ways in which mindfulness practice can literally rewire our brains and positively influence our bodies.

Brain Changes:

Reduced Amygdala Activity: The amygdala, the brain's fear center, tends to be less reactive in individuals who practice mindfulness. This translates to reduced anxiety and a greater sense of emotional balance.

Increased Prefrontal Cortex Activity: The prefrontal cortex, responsible for higher-order cognitive functions like decision-making and emotional regulation, shows increased activity with mindfulness practice. This leads to improved focus, attention, and self-control.

Thicker Gray Matter: Studies have revealed that mindfulness practice can lead to increased gray matter density in areas of the brain associated with learning, memory, emotional regulation, and self-awareness.

Enhanced Connectivity: Mindfulness strengthens the connections between different brain regions, leading to improved communication and coordination throughout the nervous system.

Physical Benefits:

Stress Reduction: Mindfulness has been shown to decrease the production of cortisol, the stress hormone, leading to a calmer and more relaxed state.

Improved Immune Function: Regular mindfulness practice has been linked to a strengthened immune response, making us less susceptible to illness.

Lower Blood Pressure: Studies suggest that mindfulness can help reduce blood pressure, contributing to a healthier cardiovascular system.

Pain Management: Mindfulness-based interventions have shown promise in reducing chronic pain and improving the quality of life for individuals with pain conditions.

Better Sleep: By calming the mind and reducing anxiety, mindfulness can contribute to improved sleep quality.

Conclusion:

The science of mindfulness is a testament to its transformative power. By training our minds to be present and non-judgmental, we can literally change the structure and function of our brains, leading to a cascade of positive effects on our physical and mental health. Whether you're seeking to reduce stress, improve focus, or simply cultivate a greater sense of well-being, mindfulness offers a scientifically proven path to a healthier and happier life.

NAVIGATING THE INNER TERRAIN

The path to mindfulness is not always smooth. As we embark on this journey of self-discovery, we inevitably encounter obstacles that can hinder our progress. Restlessness, distractions, and self-criticism are common challenges that can pull us away from the present moment and create a sense of frustration and discouragement. But with patience, understanding, and a few mindful strategies, we can navigate these inner obstacles and deepen our practice.

Restlessness:

The modern world is a breeding ground for restlessness. We're constantly bombarded with stimuli, our minds racing from one thought to the next. When we sit down to meditate or simply try to be present, this restlessness can manifest as a physical and mental agitation, making it difficult to find stillness.

Embrace the Restlessness: Instead of fighting against it, acknowledge and accept the restlessness. Notice the sensations in your body and the thoughts swirling in your mind.

Anchor Your Attention: Focus on your breath or a physical sensation, like the feeling of your feet on the ground. This will help to ground you in the present moment.

Practice Patience: Don't expect your mind to be perfectly still. It's natural for thoughts to arise. Simply observe them without judgment and gently return your attention to your anchor.

Distractions: In today's digital age, distractions are ubiquitous. From notifications on our phones to the constant stream of information online, it's easy to get pulled away from the present moment.

Create a Distraction-Free Zone: When practicing mindfulness, find a quiet space where you can minimize external distractions. Turn off your phone or put it on silent mode.

Acknowledge Distractions: When distractions inevitably arise, acknowledge them without judgment. Notice the distraction, then gently bring your attention back to your breath or chosen focus.

Practice Digital Detox: Regularly disconnect from technology to give your mind a break and cultivate greater presence in the physical world.

Self-Criticism: Our inner critic can be a formidable obstacle to mindfulness. We judge ourselves harshly for our perceived shortcomings, creating a cycle of self-doubt and negativity.

Cultivate Self-Compassion: Treat yourself with the same kindness and understanding you would offer a dear friend. Recognize that everyone makes mistakes and experiences setbacks.

Challenge Negative Thoughts: When critical thoughts arise, question their validity. Are they based on facts or assumptions? Are they helpful or harmful?

Focus on Your Strengths: Remind yourself of your positive qualities and accomplishments. Celebrate your successes, no matter how small.

Remember:

Progress, Not Perfection: Mindfulness is a journey, not a destination. Don't strive for perfection; focus on making progress and learning from your experiences.

Be Kind to Yourself: Treat yourself with compassion and understanding, especially when facing challenges.

Seek Support: If you're struggling with persistent self-criticism or other obstacles to mindfulness, consider seeking guidance from a therapist or mindfulness teacher.

By acknowledging and addressing these common challenges, you can deepen your mindfulness practice and cultivate greater peace, joy, and resilience in your life.

MINDFUL CONNECTIONS

In the intricate tapestry of human connection, mindfulness serves as a guiding thread, weaving together the strands of communication, empathy, and understanding. By cultivating present-moment awareness, we can transform our interactions with others, fostering deeper bonds and more fulfilling relationships.

Active Listening: The Foundation of Mindful Communication Mindfulness invites us to step beyond the distractions of our own thoughts and truly listen to the words and emotions being expressed by others. When we listen actively, we create a safe space for open and honest communication.

Be Fully Present: Put aside distractions and focus your full attention on the person speaking. Notice their body language, tone of voice, and underlying emotions.

Refrain from Judgment: Resist the urge to jump to conclusions or offer unsolicited advice. Instead, strive to understand the speaker's perspective without judgment.

Reflect and Clarify: Paraphrase what you've heard to ensure understanding and show that you're truly listening. Ask clarifying questions if needed.

Cultivating Empathy: Walking in Another's Shoes

Mindfulness helps us develop empathy, the ability to understand and share the feelings of others. By putting ourselves in someone else's shoes, we can bridge the gap between our own experiences and theirs.

Recognize Emotions: Pay attention to the emotions expressed by others, both verbally and nonverbally. Acknowledge their feelings without judgment.

Imagine Their Perspective: Try to imagine what it might be like to experience the situation from their point of view. Consider their background, beliefs, and values.

Offer Support: Express your understanding and offer support without trying to fix the situation or minimize their feelings.

Deepening Connection: Beyond Words

Mindfulness allows us to connect with others on a deeper level, beyond the surface of words and actions. It's about being present with the shared humanity that binds us all.

Shared Silence: Embrace moments of silence in conversations. Allow space for reflection and deeper connection.

Nonverbal Communication: Pay attention to nonverbal cues like eye contact, facial expressions, and body language. These often reveal more than words alone.

Compassionate Presence: Offer your full presence and attention to those you interact with. Let them feel seen, heard, and valued.

Mindfulness in Challenging Relationships:

Mindfulness can also be a powerful tool for navigating difficult relationships. By staying present and non-reactive, we can respond to conflict with greater wisdom and compassion.

Observe Your Reactions: Notice your own emotional triggers and patterns of reactivity. This self-awareness allows you to choose more skillful responses.

Communicate with Kindness: Express your needs and concerns clearly and respectfully, even when emotions are running high.

Set Boundaries: Establish healthy boundaries to protect your own well-being while still maintaining connection.

Remember:

Practice Patience: Cultivating mindful communication and empathy takes time and practice. Be patient with yourself and others as you learn and grow.

Lead by Example: By embodying mindfulness in your own interactions, you inspire others to do the same, creating a ripple effect of positive change.

Seek Support: If you're struggling with communication or relationship challenges, consider seeking guidance from a therapist or counselor.

By integrating mindfulness into our relationships, we can create a more compassionate, connected, and fulfilling human experience.

EMBRACING THE INNER EMBRACE

CULTIVATING SELF-COMPASSION

In the face of life's challenges, we often turn to self-criticism and harsh judgment, adding another layer of suffering to our already difficult experiences. But what if, instead of berating ourselves, we offered ourselves the same kindness and understanding we would extend to a dear friend? This is the essence of self-compassion, a practice that can profoundly transform our relationship with ourselves, particularly during times of hardship.

Understanding Self-Compassion

Self-compassion involves treating ourselves with warmth, kindness, and understanding, especially when we're struggling or feeling inadequate. It's about recognizing our shared humanity and acknowledging that everyone makes mistakes and experiences setbacks.

The Three Components Of Self-Compassion:

Self-Kindness: Instead of judging ourselves harshly, we offer ourselves warmth and understanding. We acknowledge our imperfections without condemnation.

Common Humanity: We recognize that suffering is a part of the human experience. We are not alone in our struggles, and our difficulties do not define us.

Mindfulness: We observe our thoughts and feelings with openness and non-judgment, creating space for acceptance and healing.

Cultivating Self-Compassion:

Talk to Yourself Like a Friend: When facing challenges, ask yourself, "What would I say to a dear friend in this situation?" Offer yourself the same words of encouragement and support.

Practice Mindfulness: Observe your thoughts and feelings without judgment. Notice when self-criticism arises, and gently replace it with self-kindness.

Embrace Your Imperfections: Recognize that everyone makes mistakes. Instead of dwelling on your shortcomings, focus on learning and growing from your experiences.

Prioritize Self-Care: Make time for activities that nourish your mind, body, and spirit. This might include exercise, spending time in nature, or engaging in creative pursuits.

Seek Support: Don't be afraid to reach out to trusted friends, family members, or a therapist for support and guidance.Benefits of Self-Compassion:

Reduced Stress and Anxiety: Self-compassion helps us manage difficult emotions and cope with stress more effectively.

Increased Resilience: By treating ourselves with kindness, we build inner strength and resilience in the face of adversity.

Improved Mental Health: Self-compassion has been linked to lower levels of depression, anxiety, and shame.

Enhanced Relationships: When we are kind to ourselves, we are more likely to be kind and compassionate towards others.

Remember:

Self-Compassion is Not Self-Pity: It's about recognizing your own suffering and offering yourself kindness, not wallowing in self-pity or making excuses.

Self-Compassion is Not Self-Indulgence: It's about taking care of yourself in a healthy and balanced way, not giving in to every whim or desire.

Self-Compassion Takes Practice: Like any skill, self-compassion requires practice and patience. Be kind to yourself as you learn and grow.

By cultivating self-compassion, we can create a more loving and supportive relationship with ourselves, especially during difficult times. This inner strength and resilience will empower us to navigate life's challenges with greater ease and grace.

MINDFULNESS FOR SOCIAL CHANGE

CULTIVATING COMPASSION AND ACTION

Mindfulness is often perceived as an inward-focused practice, concerned primarily with personal well-being. However, its potential for fostering social change and contributing to a more just and equitable world is profound.

By cultivating awareness, compassion, and ethical action, mindfulness can empower us to address systemic injustices and create a more harmonious society.

The Inner Work Of Social Change:

Mindfulness lays the groundwork for effective social activism by cultivating inner qualities that are essential for creating lasting change.

Self-Awareness: Through mindful self-observation, we become aware of our own biases, prejudices, and conditioned patterns of thinking. This self-awareness allows us to challenge harmful beliefs and cultivate a more inclusive and compassionate worldview.

Emotional Regulation: Mindfulness helps us manage difficult emotions like anger, fear, and despair, which can arise in the face of injustice. By cultivating emotional resilience, we can sustain our commitment to social change even in the face of adversity.

Compassion and Empathy: Mindfulness fosters a deep sense of connection to all beings, enabling us to empathize with the suffering of others and respond with compassion and care.

Mindfulness In Action:

Mindfulness not only supports our inner work but also informs our actions in the world.

Mindful Activism: By approaching activism with present-moment awareness, we can act from a place of clarity, intention, and compassion, avoiding burnout and fostering sustainable engagement.

Mindful Communication: Mindful communication allows us to listen deeply to others, understand their perspectives, and build bridges of understanding across divides.

Mindful Leadership: Mindful leaders embody qualities of integrity, compassion, and wisdom, inspiring others to work towards a more just and equitable world.

The Ripple Effect Of Mindfulness:

When individuals cultivate mindfulness, the positive effects ripple outwards, influencing families, communities, and society as a whole.

Reduced Prejudice and Discrimination: Mindfulness helps us challenge unconscious biases and cultivate greater acceptance and understanding of diversity.

Increased Social Cohesion: By fostering empathy and compassion, mindfulness strengthens social bonds and promotes a sense of interconnectedness.

Sustainable Solutions: Mindful decision-making considers the long-term impact of our actions on both people and the planet, leading to more sustainable and equitable solutions.

Conclusion:

Mindfulness is not just a tool for personal well-being; it's a catalyst for social transformation. By cultivating inner awareness, compassion, and ethical action, we can contribute to a more just and equitable world for all.

Remember:

Start with Yourself: The inner work of mindfulness is the foundation for effective social change.

Connect with Others: Engage in mindful dialogue and collaborate with others who share your vision for a more just world.

Take Action: Channel your compassion into meaningful action, whether it's volunteering, advocating for change, or simply living your values in your daily life.

By embracing mindfulness as a tool for social change, we can create a ripple effect of positive transformation, contributing to a world where compassion, justice, and equity prevail.

RECLAIMING YOUR FOCUS

MINDFUL STRATEGIES FOR NAVIGATING THE DIGITAL AGE

In today's hyperconnected world, technology has become an integral part of our lives. While it offers countless benefits and conveniences, it also poses significant challenges to our attention and well-being. The constant stream of notifications, social media updates, and information overload can leave us feeling overwhelmed, distracted, and disconnected from ourselves and the world around us.

This chapter explores mindful strategies for managing the impact of technology on our attention and well-being. By cultivating awareness and setting healthy boundaries, we can reclaim our focus, reduce stress, and create a more balanced relationship with technology.

Mindful Technology Use:

Set Intentions: Before engaging with technology, clarify your purpose and set a time limit. This will help you stay focused and avoid mindless scrolling or browsing.

Create Tech-Free Zones: Designate specific times and spaces in your day or home where technology is off-limits. This allows you to fully engage in other activities and be present in the moment.

Mindful Notifications: Turn off unnecessary notifications and declutter your digital spaces. This reduces distractions and allows you to focus on what truly matters.

Single-Tasking: Resist the urge to multitask while using technology. Focus on one task at a time to improve concentration and productivity.

Digital Detox: Take regular breaks from technology, whether it's for a few hours or a whole day. Use this time to connect with nature, engage in hobbies, or simply relax and recharge.

Mindful Social Media Use:

Curate Your Feed: Follow accounts that inspire and uplift you, and unfollow those that trigger negativity or comparison.

Limit Your Time: Set specific time limits for social media use each day. Use apps or browser extensions to track your usage and stay accountable.

Be Mindful of Your Emotions: Pay attention to how social media makes you feel. If you notice feelings of envy, anxiety, or low self-esteem, take a break or adjust your usage.

Connect in Real Life: Prioritize face-to-face interactions and meaningful conversations with loved ones.

Cultivating Healthy Digital Habits:

Mindful Phone Use: Avoid using your phone during meals, conversations, or other important activities. Be present in the moment and give your full attention to the people and experiences around you.

Mindful Email Management: Set aside specific times to check and respond to emails. Avoid constantly checking your inbox, as this can lead to distraction and stress.

Mindful Content Consumption: Be selective about the information you consume online. Choose sources that are reliable, informative, and uplifting.

Remember:

Technology is a Tool: Technology can be a powerful tool for connection, learning, and creativity. Use it mindfully to enhance your life, not detract from it.

Balance is Key: Strive for a healthy balance between online and offline activities. Make time for real-life experiences and connections.

Be Kind to Yourself: Don't judge yourself if you struggle with technology overuse. Simply acknowledge it, make adjustments, and move forward with compassion.

By implementing these mindful strategies, you can navigate the digital age with greater awareness and intention. Reclaim your focus, protect your well-being, and cultivate a more balanced relationship with technology.

UNLEASHING THE INNER CHILD

THE THERAPEUTIC POWER OF ART

In today's technologically driven world, we often find ourselves glued to screens, our eyes straining and our minds racing. But amidst the digital noise, there exists a simple yet powerful antidote: the art of creation. Engaging in mindful art offers a multitude of benefits, transforming idle time into moments of meaning and fulfillment.

From Simple to Spectacular

With readily available tools and technology, even the most basic artistic endeavors can blossom into something beautiful. The process of sketching, coloring, and experimenting with different mediums allows us to tap into our innate creativity, fostering a sense of accomplishment and satisfaction.

A Sanctuary for the Eyes

Spending hours staring at screens can take a toll on our vision and overall well-being. Engaging in mindful art provides a much-needed respite for our eyes, allowing them to relax and refocus.

Stress Buster Extraordinaire

The rhythmic strokes of a paintbrush or the gentle shading of a pencil can melt away stress and anxiety. As we immerse ourselves in the creative process, our minds quiet down, and a sense of calm washes over us.

Rediscovering the Inner Child: Art invites us to play, to experiment, and to embrace the carefree spirit of childhood. It's a chance to shed the weight of adult responsibilities and tap into the joy of pure creation.

Breathing Deeply: Feeling Joy As we lose ourselves in the act of creating, our breath naturally deepens, oxygenating our bodies and promoting a sense of relaxation. The simple act of making art can spark joy, reminding us of the inherent pleasure of self-expression.

Conclusion:

In a world that often feels chaotic and overwhelming, mindful art offers a sanctuary of peace and self-discovery. It's a chance to unplug, unwind, and reconnect with our inner child. So, pick up a paintbrush, a pencil, or any medium that speaks to you, and let the creative journey begin. You may be surprised at the profound impact it can have on your well-being.

CONCLUSION:

EMBRACING THE JOURNEY OF SELF-DISCOVERY

As we conclude this exploration of mindfulness and emotional intelligence, I hope you feel inspired and empowered to embark on your own journey of self-discovery. Remember, the path to inner peace is not a destination but an ongoing practice. By cultivating present-moment awareness, embracing your emotions with compassion, and nurturing healthy connections with yourself and others, you can navigate life's complexities with greater ease and resilience.

The tools and insights shared in this book are just the beginning. I encourage you to continue exploring the transformative power of mindfulness and emotional intelligence in your own life. May your journey be filled with moments of joy, peace, and profound self-discovery.

With gratitude and hope,

Sathyamoorthy Buma Sridhar

Mindfulness and Emotional Intellgence Coach, Mental Health Activist.

Transforming lives through mindful awareness and emotional well-being.

ABOUT THE AUTHOR

Mr. Sathyamoorthy Buma Sridhar

Mindfulness and Emotional Intelligence Coach | Mental Health Activist | Author

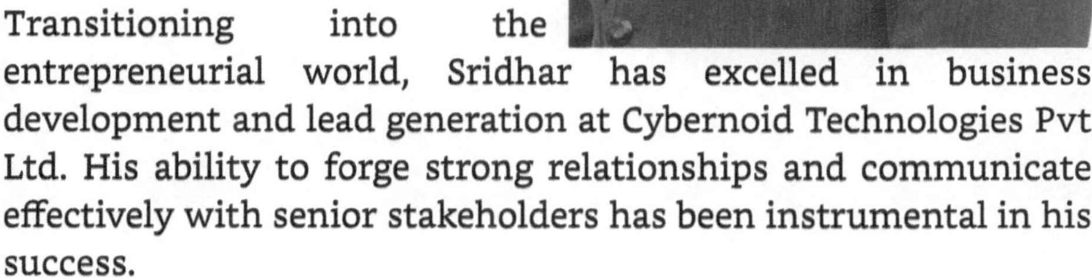

Sathyamoorthy Buma Sridhar brings a unique blend of corporate experience and mental health expertise to his work. With over 16 years in the IT industry, he has honed his skills in Quality Assurance, Business Analysis, and Agile methodologies while working with renowned organizations like HCL and Hapag Lloyd.

Transitioning into the entrepreneurial world, Sridhar has excelled in business development and lead generation at Cybernoid Technologies Pvt Ltd. His ability to forge strong relationships and communicate effectively with senior stakeholders has been instrumental in his success.

Driven by a passion for mental well-being, Sridhar is a certified Mental Health Coach and the author of "The Stillness Within" and "The Mindful Teen" He specializes in guiding individuals towards inner peace and resilience through mindfulness practices and emotional intelligence techniques.

Sridhar's multifaceted skillset encompasses brand building, social media marketing, content creation, and training. His dedication to mental health advocacy earned him recognition as a Nominee for the Best Mental Health Coach India 2021 by the Navi Mumbai Chamber of Business of India (NMCBI).

BOOKS BY THIS AUTHOR

The Mindful Teen: A Guide To Navigating Life With Awareness And Emotional Intelligence

In a world buzzing with distractions and challenges, "The Mindful Teen" provides a guide for teenagers to navigate the complexities of adolescence and cultivate a more fulfilling life. This book is a treasure trove of insights and practical strategies, addressing a wide range of relevant topics including:

Digital Well-being: Learn to manage screen time, navigate social media mindfully, and protect yourself from cyberbullying.

Relationships and Sexuality: Discover how to build healthy relationships, understand consent and boundaries, and address the impact of pornography.

Body Image and Self-Esteem: Cultivate body positivity, challenge unrealistic beauty standards, and develop healthy coping mechanisms for building self-esteem.

Stress, Anxiety, and Mental Health: Find effective ways to manage stress, anxiety, and other mental health challenges through mindfulness and emotional intelligence.

Goals, Aspirations, and Finding Your Path: Set realistic goals, manage expectations, and discover your passions while embracing a growth mindset.

With relatable anecdotes, practical exercises, and a compassionate tone, "The Mindful Teen" empowers teenagers to: Develop self-awareness and emotional intelligence: Understand and manage your emotions, build stronger relationships, and make mindful choices.

Navigate the digital world safely and responsibly: Find balance with technology, resist online pressures, and protect your well-being.

Embrace your authentic self: Cultivate self-acceptance, challenge negative thoughts, and build a positive body image.

Thrive in a competitive world: Manage academic pressure, handle competition with grace, and find joy in the process of learning and growing.

Build a supportive network: Create meaningful connections with family, friends, and mentors.

Take care of their well-being: Prioritize sleep, exercise, nutrition, and creative expression.

Seek help when needed: Recognize the signs of mental health challenges and access support resources.

"The Mindful Teen" is an invaluable resource for teenagers, parents, and educators, offering guidance and support on the journey to a more mindful, fulfilling, and emotionally intelligent adolescence.

www.ingramcontent.com/pod-product-compliance
Lightning Source LLC
Chambersburg PA
CBHW031320250726
48656CB00005B/1894